broken crowns are
still royal

Mauve Keela

BookLeaf Publishing

India | USA | UK

Presentation by *BookLeaf Publishing*

Web: www.bookleafpub.com

E-mail: info@bookleafpub.com

ISBN: 9789358314885

First edition 2023

to the love of my life, the one who told me black
was her favorite color.

nothing is sacred.

it's not okay the way you look at me
crawling all over my skin
pushing out all sacristy
trying to kiss me in dark places
is the chokehold I don't need
who told you it was okay to touch me
stroking the panic buttons in my body
igniting flight mode
switching it up by trying to save me
is the perversion that slowly kills me
it's not okay the way you move on
insinuating you're on cloud nine
tossing away your garbage
not a shred of hesitation
to the world you are golden and wise
it's not okay I lost my way
crawling inside my skin
cutting deep into all my tainted parts
clawing at the walls of my heart
to the world I am broken and weak
it's not okay that my skin is raw
all the way down to the bone
breeding new scars on top of open wounds
nothing is sacred anymore.

nicotine dreams.

empty soul
empty heart
unfulfilled needs
sex and nicotine
numb my soul
numb my heart
fill me to the brim
smoke me to the
end of senselessness

i don't want you anymore
goodbye forevermore
don't look back nor
make eye contact
leave my heart
on the floor intact
no, cracked and broken
once again i need you
but i don't want you
anymore, forevermore

leave my scars
empty my heart of
the unfulfilled greed
of nicotine dreams

in the dark of the day where
love never stays
and oceans drown me into
a sea of black and blue
where i don't need you
anymore, nevermore.

til death.

Her lips
her eyes
her skin
hands and body
the prototype
of a queen
placed upon the most high
the curl of her lip
burns through my eyes
my lips
my skin
hands and body
the way her hair is untamed
in the throes of passion
on the highest throne
of love
bears the truth that
heaven lives at home
in her deepest grasp
within her softest touch
it's a lockdown with no key
with my queen
til death
i cannot breathe.

the cycle.

5

she was born whole
until he broke her to pieces
flicked ashes on her face
hello scars of rage
she tried to live
but the price of pain
just broke her again.

truth & reality.

when you look at me
tell me what it is you see
when you hold me
tell me what it is you feel
truth is this feels like a lie
truth is it's giving
a reason to hide
so tell me when you look at me
what should i believe
and when you hold me
tell me the hopes you've conceived
reality is you really don't know
how it feels to be me
reality is you really don't know
the meaning of sincerity
so when i look at you
tell me are you real
cause when i hold you
tell me why i don't know what to feel.

the moon.

the moon never leaves
in the brightest sky she appears
in the darkest night she's there
but the world knows
when the darkness comes
that's when she really shines.

the monster.

8

he told me not to speak of foolish things
enter the bird with broken wings
the illusion of a warm and safe bed
shook by the monster asleep in my head.

the little ones.

continental divide of hate
you are erasing an unifying love
of little humans who woke with smiles
and simple desires to bask in the sun
their lessons are lost in the dark
as they woke to the horror of
today you say goodbye
today you cease to exist
today evil triumphs in your pain
your life does not matter
for you will evaporate into the wind
and blow away like dirty dust...
heavy pause.
though our hearts are broken
and our eyes stay wet
the shape of your magic will forever burn into
us,
forever.
the trees know your songs, your voices are loud
and hurricanes of leaves embody your souls,
sweet babies,
one day you'll be strong again
and the world will know your sweet revenge
the only kind you've ever known
... that of which is love.

my ocean heart.

when you were here i was engulfed in anger
unable to see
beyond the massive piers
everything tumbling down
crashing me into the ground
you were in so much pain
i couldn't see beyond the rain
the waves of pain and anger
multiplied by the years, yet you
stood there soothing my fears
when you were here i didn't smile
i didn't just fucking sit for awhile
watching from the shore, staring at the tides
the moon was never such a sore sight for my
eyes
the moon pulls my heartstrings
cursing the tides
i wish to sit at the shore side by side
as when you were here
i was unaware
your arms were open and safe
now my heart aches
crashing on the shore, where you no longer are
my anger rising to impossible heights
for when you were here

i couldn't see
my heart was dried and dead
til you left, my ocean heart then bled.

feels like home.

lift me from the toxic mire
it feels like roses under my feet
not so much a lotus
but drowning to be loved
blow me into the wind
where i can freely breathe
let me land when i feel the need
the muddy waters feel like home
numbing my soul down to the bone
a lotus flower of resonation deep within
it's the toxic mire that i know best
if only i could release and win
against sinking deep in the pits
i'd no longer crave
the murky dark love of which
i rest safely in my grave.

my angel.

my angel saved me that day
my world dark
my heart closed off
i was ready to leave
and never be found
then she came to me
so innocent and small
yet her power was mighty
the floodgates burst
my world was an ocean
my heart now hers
floating with calamity
my angel saved me
she's mine til death do us part.

brutal & benevolent.

14

the burn has been brutal
i have more than once succumbed to the pain
today someone said i mattered
a piece of my heart restored
and my soul burst aflame
no sense in taking away the brutal
for i thrive in the fire
somehow through it all, my heart stays kind
benevolence was the true lesson
mama made mine.

trust the moments.

my journey
her journey
our journey
we wake up each day
taking a leap of faith
that we will survive
returning to each other's arms
at the end of the day
the mental and emotional strength
drained each day to take this leap is insane
yet there's moments within moments
i tell her somehow we will be okay.

sinfully sweet.

cotton candy skies
hands on my thighs
deep brown eyes
tell me no lies
only sweet lullabies
starry black nights
reaching natural highs
til all that's left is the
inevitable goodbyes.

insane dreams.

when you dreamed dreams that are impossible to
reach
it's an obsession of moments that can never be
instigating a perpetual insanity
yet i can see you so clearly
hauntingly comforting
an imaginary sanctuary
where the grief is debilitating
playing a losing game
when i dream dreams that are not reality
they simply will never be
preciously chosen insanity
peace by peace
hearts fade away.

the forgotten ones.

God did you forget me?
smiles surround and swallow me
but they're not mine to keep
curled on the floor
comforted by my screams
this is how i know i am alive
but i think you forgot me
i spent my days searching for you
in every stab of trauma
in every terrorized day
i think i felt you love me once
but God where did you go?
i've needed you beyond my deepest scar
the tears water my soul down to the floor
i think you forgot
my life was never mine
please love me through and through
in the dark i never forgot you.

life and love.

there are no answers
only the day by day living
when you realize that searching
is a gifted torture we inherit
once life is near the end
the answers appear
it is not until you have completed life
that you will know if love
has completed you.

nostalgic.

i never cared to return to memories of
sweet lullabies and sinful melodies
cuz you can never go back
and relive the high
the reach without the touch
is just too sad
but now?
nostalgia haunts me all the time.

night whispers.

in my dreams i still love you
in the quiet of my thoughts
i still crave you
in the chaos of my words
i still breathe you
i hope you come to know
that in my dreams i still love you.

you know my name.

lonely called me by my name
she met me with no words
charged straight through my body
she kills with passion
and loves like she's king
a dance with the devil
the proof is in her murderous plot
of which i can no longer be queen.

broken crowns.

you on the floor, broken and torn
get up and arch that back
fix your crown
walk on strong
and don't you dare fall back
the world will break you
your deepest love will fake you
at the end of the day, there's only you
go on and fix that crown
it remains broken but true.